365 Days

And Ways

To Keep

Your Romance

Alive

Deanna L. Taber

365 Days and Ways To Keep Your Romance Alive

Copyright © by Deanna L. Taber

Cover design by Deanna L. Taber

Printed in the United States of America

April 2010

ISBN- 1452802343

EAN 13- 9781452802343

This book is dedicated to the one that continues to hold my heart.

Acknowledgment

I would like to thank everyone who gave me love and or support. Thank you for allowing me to follow my dream.

Send a dozen roses to the one you love:
11 red roses and 1 white rose.......

Enclose a note that says : "In every bunch
there's one who stands out - and you are
that one."

Write a love note to the one you love.
Insert the love note into a bottle......

Float the bottle in your love's bath water.

Call him or her at work and say.......

"Hello gorgeous! Are you free tonight?"

Send a bunch of tulips to the one you love.......

Enclose a note that says : "I have two-lips waiting for you."

Trace "I love you" on a stick of butter or margarine.......

Place the stick of butter on a plate and present it with dinner at the table.

Have pillows embroidered with your names......

Or get monogrammed pillow covers.

Hide a love note in a bottle of vitamins.....

The note should say: "Try some vitamin L."

Surprise her with a vase full of flowers......

Surprise him with a vase of flowers too.

Write love notes on Post-it notes......

Stick the Post-it notes around the house.

Toss a coin in a fountain........

Make a wish together.

Call her at work and ask: "Is this the office of the most beautiful woman in the world?"

Call him at work and ask: "Is this the office of the most handsome man in the world?"

Hide a love note in his pants pocket......

Hide a love note in her purse.

Find a four-leaf clover and present it together with a note.......

The note should say, "I got lucky when I found you."

Ask him or her to pick a number between
1 and 50.........

Reward him or her with that number of
kisses.

When dining out, share everything....

your meals and desserts.

Attach a note to the TV remote.......

The note should say,"Turn me on instead!"

Before getting out of bed, face your partner, give him or her a kiss and say.....

"I'm so thankful I have you in my life."

Attend a lousy movie, sit in the back, and ....

make out in the dark.

On your love's birthday send.......

his or her mother a "Thank you" card.

Celebrate the anniversary.....

of the day when you first met.

Shower with the one you love.....

together by candlelight.

Warm his or her bath towel in the dryer for them......

Greet them with the warmed towel after their bath.

Surprise him or her at the office.....

wearing an overcoat with nothing on
underneath.

Leave written clues that lead him or her....

to a restaurant where you are waiting for him or her.

Swing together.....

on playground swings.

Get tickets for an event.....

and keep it a secret until the day arrives.

Hide a greeting card.....

under your partner's pillow.

Surprise your partner......

at work with a single red rose.

Slip a little love note into his or her wallet..

in between the dollar bills.

Place a single rose......

under the car's windshield wiper.

Take an old prescription bottle of unused medicine capsules. Empty the medicine....

Insert tiny love notes in the bottle. Write him or her a prescription for love.

Leave a romantic message......

on the answering machine.

Eat dinner by candlelight.....

Tonight!

Put a note in a romance novel that she is reading. The note should say, "The story is great but our own love story is the best".

Put a note in a novel that he is reading. The note should say, " This story is great, but our life together has been much more epic."

Put a single red rose.....

on the seat of your lover's car before they go to work.

Leave a trail of "Hershey's chocolate kisses" from the front door to the bedroom, right up to the bed......

On the bed leave a note that reads "I kiss the ground you walk on."

Buy a romantic CD......

have it waiting in their car in the morning.

Create a photo album of pictures of the two of you......

leave the rest empty with a note that says, "to be continued."

In the middle of the week.......

ask your love out on a date to your
favorite restaurant.

E-mail or text a love quote that describes
your relationship.....

in the middle of the week.

Buy a box from a craft store......

fill it with memories the two of you share.

Try a new activity together......

learn how to ski, scuba dive or rock climb.

Lean over to your partner when they least expect it......

whisper "I love you" in their ear.

Find something you are both interested in and have never done before......

and learn how to do it together.

The next time you are out to dinner, take out a pen and write a note on a paper napkin.......

let your partner know what he or she can look forward to, when you get home.

Leave love notes in unexpected places.....

a sock drawer, the refrigerator, the medicine cabinet, car steering wheel.

If your partner is on their way home,
answer the front door.....

dressed in nothing but a smile.

Leave a note in your partner's briefcase or bag.....

the note should say "I can't wait to play later!"

Before your partner gets home.....

decorate your bedroom with candles, soft music and wine chilling in a bucket by the bedside.

Leave a love letter......

on your love's pillow before they go to
bed.

Send your love a dirty text message......

in the middle of the day.

Fulfill each others fantasies. Discuss your ultimate fantasy with your partner....

Then plan a night to make each others fantasy come true.

Meet your partner at their office at lunch.......

for an surprise picnic outside.

Fill your love's favorite coffee mug with
Hershey kisses..........

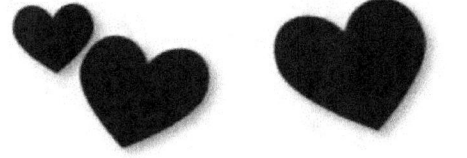

leave the mug in the cupboard where they
will find it.

Buy a Kama Sutra book....

Make a promise to try a new position at
least once a week.

Buy a pair of "special" sheets that you or your partner can put on the bed........

to silently request a romantic evening.

Arrange to meet your partner at lunchtime in the bar of a plain but presentable hotel.

Book a room, buy a bottle of champagne, and enjoy a romantic rendezvous.

When your partner gets home from work on Friday.......

tell them to pack a bag, and take them away for a romantic weekend.

Write your partner a romantic letter filled
with all the things you love about them.....

then send it to them in the mail.

Surprise your partner with a gift card to their favorite place to eat lunch......

Include a note that says, "Have lunch on me now, and later tonight have dessert "on me, too!"

On a rainy day........

have an indoor picnic with your love.

Cook your partner dinner.....

with nothing but an apron on.

Plan to not have sex for one week. You can only kiss and touch each other....

The anticipation for the weekend will drive you both wild.

Feel like a kid again.........

Go to a miniature golf course together and take your time playing mini-golf or go to an arcade and play the games.

Have a good laugh............

Take your partner to a comedy club.

Send your love a bag of candy hearts......

include a note that says this is how many
times you stole my heart.

Go to a local campground and reserve a campsite, set up a tent, fire pit, etc...

go pick up your love and surprise them with a night of cuddling by the roaring fire.

Drive around your town ....

look at Christmas lights together.

Take your partner and a loaf of bread.......

and go to a lake and feed the ducks.

Purchase a wristwatch for your partner.....

Have it inscribed with, "I always have time for you."

Attach a $100 bill to a Victoria's Secret
catalog........

attach a note that says, "You choose."

Identify a pivotal event that brought the two of you together.........

Celebrate that event every year.

Write your partner a love letter or poem on one sheet of paper. Glue it to thin cardboard, cut it up into puzzle-shaped pieces.......

mail all the pieces to him or her.

Remove all the paper strips (that say "Kisses" on them) from a couple hundred Hershey's Kisses. Fill a decorated box with them........

present them to your partner with a certificate explaining that the slips are coupons redeemable for one kiss each.

Kidnap him or her! Blindfold him or her.
Drive around town until they are
thoroughly lost.......

Then reveal your destination,a favorite
restaurant, or maybe a romantic inn.

Spend the entire day..........

cuddling and watching romantic movies.

Instead of waiting for the weekend for a date..........

Call your partner from work midweek and formally ask for a date.

Call a local radio station.........

request a special love song to be dedicated
to your partner.

Mail your partner a Rolodex card with your name and number on it........

Write on it: "Your resource for love. Call when lonely."

Write "I love you" ....

on the bathroom mirror with a piece of soap.

When out together in public.......

wink at your partner from across the room.

Bring home one........

small unexpected gift each week.

Give a full-body massage......

unexpectedly.

Pick wildflowers on the way home......

and present them to the one you love.

Prepare strawberries with fondue chocolate......

and feed them to your partner.

Read poetry...............

together.

Send a love email...........

every day.

Buy some good wine, grab a couple of blankets..........

and watch shooting stars together.

Take a bath together..........

Don't forget the bubbles.

Make a list of everything you love about
him or her.........

and present it to him or her.

Clip or email things that make you think of him or her.......

every day.

Paint each other with flavored body paint...

Be creative!

If your partner is going away for a few days, tell him or her that you are worried about them, so you have organized a bodyguard to look after them.

Then give him or her a teddy bear to take with them.

Buy a package of glow in the dark stars
stick the stars on the ceiling above your bed......

to spell out a message such as "I Love
You."

Write love notes on..........

the eggs in his or her refrigerator.

Mail him or her a pack of matches....

include a note that says, "I'm hot for you."

Write love notes............

on a roll of toilet paper.

Write romantic reminders...........

on his or her to do list.

While he or she is asleep.....

place a greeting in front of his or her alarm clock.

Buy your partner eleven real red roses and one artificial red rose......

Place the artificial rose in the center of the bouquet. Attach a note that says:
"I will love you until the last rose fades."

On a weekday, get up really early........

and go out for breakfast with the one you love.

When the one you love is sick at home,

take a day off to look after him or her.

Give the one you love a magic gift box.

Every month, place a new small gift in the box for him or her to discover.

Rent the movie, "An Affair To Remember".

Buy some popcorn, champagne and
chocolate covered strawberries and have a
special movie night at home.

If the weather is warm, find a secluded spot near a beach or lake......

go for an impromptu skinny dip with your partner.

Spend a leisurely afternoon with the one you love in a large book shop such as Barnes and Noble .....

where you can browse the shelves, share a coffee and sit down to peruse your purchases.

Make homemade notes, add some with sexual innuendo....

in his or her lunchbox.

Cut out favorite cartoons, from the local
paper......

that are of interest to him or her.

Surprise the one you love ....

by having a photo of him or her
professionally painted onto canvas!

Give the one you love a small box. On the inside flap write "Just 50 of the many reasons why I love you."

Have 50 strips of paper inside with various reasons why you love him or her.

Drive into the country, find a grassy hill and lie with the one you love......

look up at the clouds. Look for shapes in the cloud formations.

Leave a long stem rose where the one you love will find it.....

attach a note saying: "Thank you for coming into my life."

Organize a professional photo shoot to obtain a portrait of the two of you as a couple....

Frame the picture and put it somewhere prominent.

Organize a mystery trip for you and the one you love.....

Talk to a travel agent to see if they will organize a mystery package where the destination of your trip is kept secret until you are actually on the plane or arrive at the destination.

If the one you love is going on a trip......

pack a small present into the corner of his or her suitcase that he or she will find when they are away.

Buy a tree with the one you love and plant it in a special spot....

On your anniversary, have a glass of wine next to your tree and talk about how your love and the tree have grown.

On a warm summer night, organize a
backyard picnic. Spread a blanket on
the ground and munch on some snacks,
like chocolates and champagne.....

Lie down on the blanket with your partner
and gaze up at the stars together.

Photocopy your hand and fax a copy of it to your partner........

include a message that says, "Do you want to hold hands?"

Order a pizza, ask to have it cut into a
heart shape.......

before it is delivered to your home.

Rent a tandem bike and go for a ride with the one you love.

At the end of your ride have a picnic in the park.

Buy the one you love a gold fish in a bowl and give it to him or her with a card that says.......

"Of all the fish in the sea, you're the fish for me!"

Buy the domain name of the one you love's name if it is available. Create a web page that contains a romantic poem and a picture of a rose.

The next time your partner is surfing the web, casually ask whether they have ever checked to see whether their domain name is taken. Let him or her type it in to discover their page.

If the one you love has a pet that he or she adores, at Christmas.....

purchase a gift for the one you love and a small present for his or her pet.

If you shower first in the morning. Steam up the bathroom........

and write a message on the mirror for your partner to read when he or she uses the bathroom.

When the one you love is sitting at a table or desk, come up behind him or her and give them a back or shoulder massage.....

finish with a gentle kiss on the cheek.

Go to the drive in movies......

instead of sitting in the car, spread a
blanket on the ground. Cuddle with the
one you love and enjoy the movie.

Arrange a day off from work. Start
with breakfast, go for a walk in the park,
go shopping........

finish off with a romantic dinner with the
one you love.

Put store bought valentines, or comical
cards.......

in his or her lunchbox.

At Halloween.......

carve "His" and "Hers" jack-o-lanterns.

Purchase some mistletoe and hang it over
your door......

every time your loved one comes
home, stand under it, kiss them, and let
them know how much you love them!

Print off a classic love poem........

leave it somewhere for him or her to find.

Write down random questions on slips of paper......

spend an afternoon choosing slips and answering them.

Send the one you love an email or a text at work saying......

"Guess what I won't be wearing when you get home?"

Go out for the evening........

tell everyone you're on your honeymoon.

Take a hike together.......

carve your initials in a tree.

Do the dishes together......

then apply hand lotion to each others
hands.

Play Romantic Word Scrabble. Play Scrabble as usual.....

you may only use words that relate to love, sex, romance and relationships.

Get your adrenaline pumping.....

take a test-drive of a fun sports car with
the one you love.

Dig out your old concert T-shirt.....

take the one you love to his or her favorite rock band concert.

Buy a hand mirror and give it to the one you love as a gift....

Include a card in the box that says,
"In this mirror you will see the image of the most gorgeous person in the world."

When the one you love has had a really long hard day.........

run a hot bath for him or her. Pour some fragrant bath oil into the tub and gently bathe him or her from head to toe.

Go for a walk on the beach. Trace out the
shape of a large love heart in the sand.....

Sit inside the heart and cuddle the one you
love as you watch the sun go down.

Be adventurous ....

go tubing together down a local river.

Take the one you love to a nearby river or
stream and race rubber ducks.....

the loser takes the winner out for dessert.

Buy a set of matching silk pajamas......

take turns modeling them for each other.

Leave a message like "I love you" on your partner's phone calendar.....

Set an alarm for when you know you won't be together the alarm will remind them that he or she is on your mind.

Don't wear underwear......

and let the one you love find out.

Share a talent with your mate.....

sing to them or give them a painting or
poetry by you.

If your partner is starting a new job, buy a copy of "The Sound Of Music" sound track.

Tape the song, "I Have Confidence" onto a CD and add your own message at the end of the song saying, "Good Luck, I   I have confidence in you.

If the one you love is going to work and you are staying at home say goodbye to him or her at the front door after they leave.....

send an email to his or her work address. The email should simply say, "Miss you already".

If you are walking by a park, visit the swings ....

and swing together.

Invite your partner to go for a walk. Pack a backpack with items for lunch......

When you find a romantic spot, ask if he or she would like to stop for a bite to eat.

Contact you love's family and ask if
there was anything he or she always
wanted when they were little.....

Go out and buy the item and present it to
him or her on their birthday.

Organize a hot air balloon trip.....

and surprise the one you love with a float
over the countryside.

Purchase a box of chocolates and carefully open one side of the plastic wrap so that you can slide the box out....

Open the box and place a love note inside. Then slide the box back into its plastic wrap and reseal it.

Talk to your partner's family and find out what his or her favorite book was when he or she was a little......

Buy a copy of the book and read it to him or her in bed.

Have a fondue party with the one you love.....

use chocolate sauce, strawberries,cherries, and whipped cream. Then smother him or her with sweet, chocolate kisses.

If your love's favorite sports team is in town......

surprise him or her with two tickets.

Listen to classical music......

and cuddle in the dark or with candles lit.

If you have access to a spa, create a romantic atmosphere by placing some candles around the tub and some rose petals floating on the surface of the water.

As the one you love enjoys the water, serve champagne and chocolate covered strawberries before joining him or her.

Buy a book that you and your love are both interested in reading.....

Take turns reading one chapter out loud each night in bed.

Hide a bunch of silly prizes and a card.....

in your partner's favorite cereal.

Use chalk to write a welcome home
message......

on the sidewalk.

Ride a city's entire public rail transit system......

go out on remote branch lines, just for fun.

Create a dinner of miniature foods with the one you love....

eat dinner on small plates.

Create a childlike picture with a smiley sun and two stick figures holding hands. Add labels with your two names pointing to the stick figures. Write "I Love You" inside a heart.....

Place the drawing inside a formal looking envelope and address it with your partners name and work address. Mail it to your partner so he or she receives it in the middle of their day.

When you and your partner are enjoying a restful trip out of town......

decide to wake up early one morning and go to a scenic spot to watch the sun rise.

Buy a kite with two hand lines and on a
windy day find a park.......

and fly the kite with the one you love.

If the one you love is sick.......

rent some videos, make him or her some soup, wrap him or her up in a blanket and just be with them.

Line a delicate trail of rose petals along the bed.......

place a love letter atop a mound of the rose petals.

Write a note saying "I thought of you today, and it made me smile."

Leave the note somewhere where the one you love is sure to find it.

Go for a hike.....

After a day of hiking, build an open fire. Sit by the fire with the one you love and toast marshmallows.

Make a couple's website dedicated to one you love.

Fill up the website with pictures, poems and blurbs about how much they mean to you.

Look up the date of the next meteor
shower......

and send the one you love a letter covered
in stars inviting them to join you.

Give the one you love.....

a picture of you to keep in their wallet or purse.

Attend a farmers' market with the one you love......

purchase items for dinner. Go home and prepare the meal together.

Book a double massage for yourself and the one you love.......

at a fancy spa.

Find out if a nearby wine store throws free wine tastings......

take the one you love to taste some wine.

Take a kissing challenge.....

Try kissing 100 times in three hours.

Whisper "I Love You" lightly in his or her ear.......

when they least expect it.

Make his or her coffee.......

so it is ready when he or she gets up.

Get dancing!

Sign you and the one you love up for
Tango lessons.

Purchase or borrow an easy-to-operate remote-control plane.......

go to a park and take turns trying to avoid the trees.

Hold the one you love during a
thunderstorm........

tell them that your heart beats louder than
that for him or her.

When the one you love has to work late,
create a late night survival lunch box

and fill it with some of his or her favorite
edible things.

When you and your partner are in a mall or airport, stop at one of those instant photo booths......

Choose a romantic background and kiss the one you love while the photo is being taken.

While having dinner one night, the one you love about the things he or she has always wanted to do......

over time try and help make them happen.

Purchase a small decorated cardboard box, a sheet of colored tissue paper, some massage oil and a blank card.....

Line the box with the tissue paper. Place the massage oil in the box and write the following message on the card:

I know a great Masseuse.
For an appointment ring:
(Your Phone Number)

Research your partner's favorite hobby and purchase a gift....

that is really useful for his or her hobby.

Use a bathroom crayon and write your love
a message all over the shower walls.....

the message won't show up until he or she
takes a shower!

Write on the sticky side of a Post It Note a little love note....

Attach the note to the bottom of your partner's drinking glass. When they get to the bottom of their glass or when they look through the clear liquid, they will see your love note.

Spend the night in your guest room.....

Pretend that you and the one you love are
on a romantic vacation.

Write the reasons you love your partner on balloons.........

and leave the balloons in their house, car or tied to their bike.

Send the one you love a message
saying....

"I love you" in different languages.

Camp "out" inside......

watch movies based on an outdoors
theme, cook S mores in the microwave,
and eat hotdogs.

Change the desktop or laptop image.......

to something that will make them laugh or think of you.

If the one you love has voice mail at work or on his or her mobile, leave a message saying.......

"Just wanted to let you know that I'm thinking of you."

Place an ad in the paper on a regular day
say something like.....

Dear John (Jane), With you by my side,
everyday feels like Valentines Day.
T hank's for being you. Love, John (Jane)

Compliment the one you love in public....

If you are in a group setting and it is appropriate to the conversation say something like, "John (Jane) makes the most incredible lasagna."

Purchase some rose petals and place them behind the sun visor on the passenger side of your car.....

Write on a post it note, "I Love You" and stick it to the back of the sun visor. As you are driving, look at your partner and tell him or her they have a mark on their cheek. They will pull down the sun visor to use the mirror and be showered in rose petals and see your love note.

Take the one you love on a cruise.......

a whale-watching cruise.

Create your own version of trick-or-treating.......

Put on a sexy outfit and knock on his or her office door.

Pick up a bucket of fried chicken......

and go to a drive-in movie.

Listen for things that your partner reminisces about and write them down somewhere.......

When a special occasion comes along, try to recreate one of the memories, for him or her.

Fill the trunk of your car with helium balloons. Drive to a romantic spot in the country to go for a walk.......

Ask the one you love to grab something out of the trunk. When they open the trunk the balloons will be released.

On a hot summers day, purchase two large water pistols and take them to the beach with you....

Pull the water pistols out and throw one to the one you love and have a water fight.

Go to church with the one you love......

and worship together.

Frame a picture of you together......

and present it to the one you love.

What's your partner's favorite cookie?

Bake a batch of his or her favorite cookies.

Create a collage by collecting some photographs of you and the one you love, some ticket stubs of places you have visited and any other small odds and ends that have special meaning.....

buy a frame and for your creation and present it to the one you love.

Send a text in secret code that you have worked out before.......

Use numbers like 1123 (could be the day you met), 214 (valentines), etc.

Rent a limo......

and take the one you love out on the town
for the night.

Create some love coupons that the one you love can exchange for romantic favors.

Use a date many years in the future as an expiration date.

Spend an evening without the TV on with the lights off and candles lit....

ask each other questions and get to know one another better.

Go to a dollar store and purchase some inexpensive gifts "just because"......

and put them together in a small box with a ribbon. Present it to the one you love.

At the beach write I love you in the sand
and take a picture of it......

frame the picture and hang it as a
reminder of how much you love each
other.

Bring home your favorite fast food........

but serve it on your best china. Don't forget the candles.

Find a fountain and throw in 10 pennies....

taking turns making wishes with the one you love.

Hold a kiss with the one you love.....

for one elevator ride.

Take the one you love to a batting cage....

and swing at some balls together.

Leave a Hershey's Kiss and a note where it will be found by the one you love. The note should say.........

"I'm thinking of kissing you."

Take the one you love out on......

a rowboat out on a lake at sunset.

Go for a Ride with the one you love......

rent a Vespa.

Leave a some bananas on the kitchen
table with a note that says:

"I go bananas over you!"

Buy 11 white tulips and 1 red roses. Send them to the one you love with the following note:

"In every group there is one so pretty, that they stand out from the crowd."

Pick a special night, dim the lights and put on soft music......

and undress leaving a trail of your clothes from the front door to the bedroom, before the one you love arrives home.

Write "I'm hot for you" in the steam.......

on the bathroom mirror.

Make a heart-shaped bookmark.....

and place it in your partners book that
they are reading.

Buy an carved wooden box that is lined with green or red felt. Find an old fashioned key and place it in the box......

Next, get a small gold plaque and have it engraved with the words "The Key To My Heart." Fix the plaque to the inside of the top of the box so that it can be read when the box is opened.

The day before your love's birthday buy some helium balloons and streamers and hide them in a closet.......

When the one you love has fallen asleep, string the streamers around the room and bring out the balloons. Place them around the bed so that your partner wakes up to a birthday surprise.

Write a story about when you first met the one you love. Or when you were first together........

Write down how you felt the moment you met, and how things have become even more amazing since you first met.

Send the one you love a love letter......

with a return address of only, "Your Secret Admirer."

Explore a wild and scenic place you've
always wanted to check out......

with the one you love.

Create a romantic atmosphere hang white Christmas lights around your house and dim the lamps.......

Play slow music on your stereo and dance with the one you love.

Share your food with the one you love.....

When you go out for a meal, hold a forkful up to his or her mouth and say, "You've got to try this."

Fulfill one of your love's teenage
fantasies.......

borrow or rent a convertible and go for a
moonlit ride.

Spend a day together visiting different places around town.......

taking pictures of each other.

Find a rarely-used corner in your library.....

Steal a few hot kisses from the one you love.

Take a night-time walk with the one you love........

to look at your neighborhoods holiday decorations and lights.

Go to an interesting location like a gazebo, or park........

and order a pizza.

Unravel a ball of yarn throughout the whole house, with little treats and cards along the way......

make the best prize at the end.

Grab the one you love and a pair of binoculars......

spend an afternoon bird-watching.

If you have kids, organize a weekend trip to their grandparents.....

On Friday night, tell the one you love that the weekend is yours and start planning how you are going to spend your special time together.

One night turn off the TV and put the
laptop to sleep.......

spend the evening telling the one you love
exactly why you fell in love with him or her
and what you love about him or her today.

Write down the story of how you first met- or a memorable first date......

and frame it for the one you love.

Find a wild berry patch.......

enjoy picking and eating berries with the
one you love.

Borrow or purchase a telescope.......

and head out for some stargazing with the one you love. Make sure to pack a blanket.

Challenge yourself and the one you love to come up with the best/worst movie he or she has ever seen......

watch them both if you can stand it and award a small prize, such as a back rub, to the winner.

Go camping with the one you love......

and only take one sleeping bag.

Go to the airport with the one you love....

and watch the planes.

Look through old photo albums with the you love........

and tell each other stories of your childhood.

Blindfold the one you love and feed them
Jelly Bellies jelly beans......

If they guess the flavor correctly, they get
a prize. If they guess wrong, you get a
prize.

252

Set up a taco bar with all the fixings or.....

make homemade pizza with the one you love.

While relaxing at home one night, take two large sheets of paper and some pencils or crayons. On each paper, draw the outline of a large crystal ball sitting on a stand.....

Tell the one you love to look into their crystal ball and draw what they see five years in the future. Do the same thing yourself and then come together to share and discuss your drawings.

Write the one you love a steamy email, describing what you want to do with them, but don't finish.......

sign with "to be continued the next time we meet."

Go to a card store with the one you love and read greeting cards......

Show each other the ones you would give.

Park your car in a secluded place and make out with the one you love like you are in high school.......

fog up those windows, baby!

Instead of dinner, go out for dessert.....

Find a cozy restaurant with a romantic
atmosphere, and share a slice of
cheesecake or a slice of chocolate cake.

Send the one you love......

a sexy picture of you.

If it is raining outside create a play day
with the one you love.....

rent movies, cook breakfast together in
your pajamas and stay in them all day.

Purchase disposable cameras.......

go sight-seeing in your own town with the one you love.

Grab a latte with the one you love....

and walk down main street together.

Bury a time capsule with the one you love
with trinkets and love letters to each other.
Draw a map with an X marking the spot....

dig it up in 10 or 20 years.

Purchase advertising space on a billboard sign on your partner's route to work......

and declare your love to the one you love.

Create a loving nickname for the one you love......

and use it often.

Serve the one you love breakfast in bed.
Try the following.....

a poached egg in the shape of a heart,
french toast with cinnamon and maple
syrup.

Purchase a coloring book and crayons. Go outside with the one you love, spread a blanket on the ground......

and color like little kids. Frame your art work and display it.

Purchase the ingredients for ice cream
sundaes.......

and create ice cream sundaes with the one
you love.

Frame a picture of the two of you together, on the back of the photo......

write a sexy message! The one you love will know the message is there but they can keep the photo in public.

269

Go for a helicopter ride over your town.....

with the one you love.

Write the one you love a love letter......

use kiddie stickers that say things like
"terrific'" or "you're great."

Make a romantic dinner with the one you love......

and serve it on your finest china.

Pick the one you love up for a date and blindfold him or her before driving to a special destination.........

make the destination something really unexpected like a table set up at the top of a cliff or a dinner on a boat.

Take a day off from work........

and plan the day with the one you love.

Download a map of your state (or your county if you live in a big state), you and the one you love each close your eyes, and point your finger to a random place on the map.....

then decide whose location looks more interesting, and plan a day trip or weekend getaway there.

Have a really big pillow fight with the one you love....

buy two pillows that are filled with feathers. Put holes in the pillows so the feathers will start to fly and then attack the one you love when the time is right.

Give the one you love a written bill after dinner.....

"Salad: One kiss. Entree: Eight kisses. Dessert: Three kisses.

Be playful with the one you love.....

Build a fort like little kids do using blankets, chairs and pillows. Turn off all the lights and light a few candles.

Visit a specialty food factory with the one you love........

such as a chocolate factory.

Take the one you love to a midnight cult
movie, like........

The Rocky Horror Picture Show or
Showgirls .

Buy the one you love a letter opener. Then over a course of four days give them four letters..........

The first letter is for a dinner date. The second letter has a tape or written love songs. The third letter has movie tickets. The fourth letter is a note saying, "I love you."

Write a message with the one you love and tie it to a balloon (or send it off in a bottle)......

Ask whoever finds it to mail you the message and tell you where they found it.

Get involved as a couple, in a project to help others.....

such as volunteer at a soup kitchen.

Buy season tickets to the performing arts group of his or her choice.......

dress in your finest, go to a romantic restaurant together, and enjoy the evening.

Go apple picking with the one you love.....

and make an apple pie with the apples.

Send a gift basket of indulgent items......

to the one you love.

Take the one you love to dinner and ......

do some stargazing at the planetarium's evening show.

Take the one you love to a paint-your-own-
pottery place.......

and paint some coffee mugs together.

Take the one you love to hit some balls.....

at the golf-ball driving range.

Take the one you love for......

a horseback-riding lesson.

Find creative places to write "I Love You"
to the one you love.........

carved into the side of an apple or in whip
cream on a slice of pie.

Feed the one you love........

make a dinner and eat with no plates or utensils.

Send the one you love a letter from "a secret admirer" who wishes to get together with them in a private spot for some adult fun......

leave an address and time for them to meet you, and tell them to not wear underwear.

Invite the one you love over (have him or her bring their laptop), and sit side-by-side on the couch. Play games online against each other........

invent some of your own rules - for example, if you lose a round, you have to remove a piece of clothing.

In a traffic jam or waiting for the light to turn green.........

lean over and give a kiss to the one you love.

Pay a skywriter to declare your love......

in the sky for all to see.

Write a thank you note to the one you love for.......

all the things you take for granted.

Surprise the one you love with........

twenty six gifts from A-Z.

Take the one you love to the nearest race track.......

to check out the action.

Create a beer garden at home with the one you love.....

look in local stores for unusual beers and taste them.

Plant a tree with the one you love.....

talk about how you will carve your names
in it with a heart in twenty years.

Create a special email account for you and your love. Use both of your first names as the account name. Use a password like "forever." Send an email to the account with links to pictures about love......

Give the one you love a card with the account info.

On a snowy day.....

make snow angels with the one you love.

Make a giant chocolate chip cookie in a pizza pan. Decorate and wrap in clear plastic. Attach ribbons and balloons.....

Leave it by your love's front door. Use a cell phone, to tell the one you love to look on their front porch.

Take a tour with one you love......

of the house you would love to own.

Take the one you love to an ice skating rink ....

and strap on skates for some fun on ice.

Take the one you love to sample
international food........

at a street fair.

Take an adventurous road trip with the one you love......

Flip a coin (heads=yes, tails=no) and ask it random questions such as, "Should we turn right here?" "Should we pull over and kiss?"

Tie a card or gift on a three foot string and tie it to the bottom of an automatic garage door.......

When your love comes home, the gift will magically rise to greet them.

Play in the snow with the one you
love.....

have a snowball fight, build snow forts or
snowmen,or have a snow sculpture
contest.

Take the one you love for a ride......

a hay ride or horse-drawn carriage ride.

Spend a few extra minutes together in bed with the one you love.......

each morning.

Have some five star fun with the one you love.......

dress up your backyard picnic table with a white tablecloth,add candles, fancy cheese, and chocolate.

Have a mystical time with the one you love......

get your palms read.

Go out of town for the weekend with the one you love......

and tell people your on honeymoon, even if your not.

Hide love notes for the one you love......

in their favorite magazines.

Dig up some dirt with the one you love.....

plant a garden together.

Hide your love's favorite candy......

in his or her coat pockets.

Wrap the bed you share with your love.....

with ribbon and a big bow.

Tape your favorite TV show.....

and spend the evening talking with the
one you love.

Get the one you love to write out five of his or her fantasies on pieces of paper and you do the same......

when you are both finished, put the ten fantasies in a jar and keep it in a private place. Take turns picking from it whenever the time is right.

Get educated together.......

sign up for a one-night class at your local college with the one you love.

Act like kids together......

climb a tree, catch lightening bugs, feed some ducks, blow bubbles.

Make breakfast for the one you love......

make heart-shaped cinnamon toast for
breakfast.

Make a Christmas ornament......

with a picture of you and the one you love
for the Christmas tree.

Buy a stuffed animal just because......

and give it to the one you love.

Go restaurant hopping with the one you love.....

start things off with cocktails and appetizers at a lounge. Then go somewhere new for the main course. Finish up at a cozy restaurant, where you can get coffee and dessert.

Take the one you love to a festival......

a food festival, jazz festival or wine
festival.

Do something completely out of character
with the one you love.....

something you ordinarily wouldn't be
caught dead even thinking about.

Skip stones with the one you love....

on a lake.

Head to the highest point in town with the one you love.......

spend an early evening watching the twinkling lights turn on.

Write a poem together.......

with the one you love.

Spend a few minutes making out in the car with the one you love.......

after a date, instead of going straight inside.

Stash a love note..........

in your love's shoe.

Build a snow fort together......

with the one you love.

Place a love note for the one you love.....

in the personals section of the newspaper.

Go to a busy place like an airport, a mall or a public square and sit down together to watch the people.......

Make up stories about who they are and where they're going.

Make a handmade gift,not for any special
occasion......

but because you love him or her.

Declare your love ....

with a telegram.

Take a taxi and play around-the-world cocktails......

Sample one specialty drink from a wine bar, one from a pub, and another from a Russian vodka room.

Order a custom-made cake for the one you love with.......

"I love you" written on it.

Share an ice cream or milkshake with the one you love.......

use two straws or two spoons.

Ride the train with the one you love to a nearby town......

do a walking tour, eat lunch, shop and ride the last train of the day back home.

Put together a little gift on his or pillow.....

include chocolate and a note that says, "Your love is like chocolate: sweet and delicious."

Create a romantic dinner.......

bring home great take-out food, and light some candles.

Find a hotel that has a jacuzzi......

and book a room for a one night getaway
for you and the one you love.

Write down twenty things you love about him or her.......

and slip it under his or her dinner plate.

Take an interest in your love's interests.....

watch a football game or see a chick-flick.

Write notes on future dates in your love's date book.......

"I love you," "I miss you," etc.

Play strip poker with the one you love....

make it more interesting by making the chips worth kisses, romantic treats, and more when they're cashed in.

In the summer time......

jump through sprinklers with the one you love.

Set up a simple picnic on the beach.......

and give the one you love a call to join you.

Give the one you love a back rub, try spelling secret messages with your finger and see if he or she can guess what you wrote........

take turns and see who gets more right.

Make a date with the one you love, to meet for lunch or dinner......

and pretend it's a blind date.

Play a rousing game of Twister with the
one you love......

play it naked.

Go for a cheap date with the one you
love.....

find a bar with happy hour, 10-cent wings
and two-dollar draft beers.

Choose a favorite photo of you and the one you love as a couple.....

frame two copies, one for each of you to take to work.

Play dress up with the one you love......

Take digital photos of each other in fancy clothes and costumes.

Do brunch and a matinee......

with the one you love.

Give the one you love a shave or facial.....

let him or her return the favor.

Write down fifty favorite memories of your life spent together with the one you love...

invite your love to add to the list.

Rent movies with the one you love.....

watch the movies and snuggle naked
under covers.

Take the one you love on a cruise.......

make it a dinner cruise.

Order live lobsters, plop them in a pot.....

and have a beach party with the one you love at home.

Drive the one you love up the wall......

at an indoor climbing gym.